JOURNEYS WITH JERRY

A PICTORIAL STORY OF MY YEARS WITH JERRY LEWIS

BY JOE PROULX

WITH SHIRLEY PROULX

Copyright © 2015 Joe Proulx
Sedona, AZ
shirleyjproulx@gmail.com

All rights reserved. No part of this book may be reproduced in any form or by any electronic or mechanical means, including information storage and retrieval systems, without permission in writing from the author.

Photographs graciously provided by Jerry Lewis as well as Joe and Shirley Proulx.

Book design by Shirley Proulx, Naomi C. Rose, and Erica Patstone
Text set in Garamond

ISBN-13: 978-0-692-48901-7

Printed in United States

DEDICATED TO

Cap'n. Queeg, my special name for a cherished friend and employer JERRY
LEWIS. He added many challenges, as well as pleasure to my years.

- Joseph (Joe) Proulx

Joe and Jerry, 1958.

PREFACE

In 1996, *San Diego Magazine's* Tom Blair asked Jerry Lewis when I was going to write my book . . . in other words, "spill the beans." Jerry told him I had been working for him since 1959, and that "Joe would never write a book 'cause he's my friend."

I'm writing this book not to "spill the beans," but to share my wonderful years with Jerry in pictures and prose. It's a "happy feel-good" book full of his kindness and consideration. He gave me the opportunity to have a meaningful career instead of just "taking home a paycheck" and joining others who go through their working lives in boredom and frustration. I was spared that, and I'm eternally grateful. I wish I could do it again! A friend suggested I share some of these thoughts and pictures as an insight into my Cap'n. Queeg, an endearing title I call Jerry.

I agreed to try to capture the essence of our years together, but please remember I am 91 years old. Time has dimmed many memories, and I find some dates, names, and places are elusive. Please excuse any errors I may make. In the early days of my employment, there are few really good photos to go with my story. Jerry had a Polaroid camera, and some of the pictures are those he gave me 50 or more years ago.

I would like to acknowledge the generosity of Jerry Lewis, who approved my writing about our "yachting" days and furnished many of the pictures with *carte blanche* to use them as I wished. They were treasured through the years, and my hope is that they provide the reader with pleasure and insight.

I cherish the essence of our relationship and lives together. As I write this, Cap'n. Queeg, please know I will always be your Friend.

- Joe

Jerry Lewis

SEPTEMBER 10TH, 2014

TO: JOE PROULX

DEAR JOE,

    I LOVED GETTING YOUR LETTER. I LOVE THE IDEA OF THE BOOK. I'M ALL IN FOR WHATEVER YOU NEED OR WANT AND I'M SURE IT WILL BE TERRIFIC.

    MY LOVE TO SHIRLEY.

ALWAYS,

Jerry

JERRY

THE EARLY YEARS 1

Jerry owned two yachts during 1959 to 1966, *Pussycat*, and a second *Pussycat*. At the time, Jerry and I had young families. He was married to Patti and had six sons. I was married to Louise, and had five children, one son and four daughters. I would like to acknowledge Louise's support while I worked for Jerry during those years. It couldn't have been easy to raise small children while her husband was gone at all hours, and on important family days.

Jerry, too, was "over the top" with demands on his time and talent. He fulfilled many roles, and it's hard to imagine how he covered so much ground as actor, director, husband and father. Patti had her hands full with all the demands of a large family and home, and she occasionally brought the children onto the boats for weekend visits.

During his yachting days, Jerry used his boats for pleasure, and as a haven from his hectic schedule. He often welcomed guests for entertainment and business. All of his yachts were docked in San Diego Bay. He lived in Bel Air and commuted from Los Angeles by air, whenever possible.

THE BELLBOY: This is the Chris Craft that Jerry bought, and named after one of his films. It began his love of boating, water-skiing, and San Diego. Being an excellent water-skier, he soon discovered the joy awaiting him "on the water."

One weekend Jerry and Joe Stabile, his manager and good friend, were enjoying a day of water-skiing, and stopped to eat a sandwich. Jerry remarked how much better his tuna sandwich tasted on the water. Then, he thought, "wouldn't it be great if I could enjoy the comforts of home, and still be on the water, with a shower, and a place to sleep."

The Bellboy.

Not being one to let grass grow under his feet, Jerry took Joe Stabile and *The Bellboy* over to the Chris Craft dealer on Shelter Island, and immediately bought a new 41' Chris Craft Constellation. This yacht offered him all the comforts he was looking for. *The Bellboy* was his runabout and ski boat. He christened his new yacht *Pussycat*, and so began a love affair with San Diego waters, that would last a lifetime.

Jerry's 41-foot Chris Craft Constellation *Pussycat*.

The yacht had a salon, one master stateroom, a galley, two heads, (bathrooms), and crew's quarters.

One day Jerry came up to me in the boat yard of the Chris Craft dealer and said, "Joe, you're always working on my boat. Why don't you come to work for me full time?" I didn't hesitate. "Sure, I'd like that!" I was now the Captain of Jerry's yacht. These few words began a relationship that was to last for many years, and provide me with a unique career with the famous star, Jerry Lewis.

Jerry loved to cruise beautiful San Diego Bay. I sat next to him and noticed he had a "heavy foot" so to speak, and opened the gas throttle full ahead. He loved to "dock" the boat, and he did a first class job of it!

Jerry usually had his meals at a nice restaurant in town, and never considered leaving me alone on board – I joined him every time. What fun! So many people wanted autographs and pictures with him, it was often hard to finish a meal. At times, the seekers could be a challenge – rude and demanding.

Joe and Jerry aboard *Pussycat*.

Patti asked me how much I was being paid by the Chris Craft Dealer, and I told her. She said "you're being paid twice that much now!" What a great way to start a new job.

Joe.

The first few months I kept busy installing new radio equipment, radar, and navigational aids. Having a background as a shipwright, plus my Master's U.S. Coast Guard's License, let me function in almost any capacity. This background served me well as I began to turn *Pussycat* into the vessel Jerry valued. I also kept a protective eye on his new "toy."

Jerry and Patti topside on the forward deck of *Pussycat*.

These were the years Jerry was making films at a breakneck pace; his schedule was frantic, and the ability to "escape" to the water haven that San Diego offered was "just what the doctor ordered."

Jerry and Patti topside.

For Joe
from the
family of the
"Pussy cat"
1/65

Patti and Jerry's 1964 Christmas Card.

Some weekends Jerry would bring one or two of his sons with him to San Diego. His eldest son, Gary (top row, right) was a young "wannabe" entertainer, and later formed the band Gary Lewis and The Playboys.

Joe Stabile (far right) was Jerry's manager and was often with him on his trips to San Diego. We shared many enjoyable times together, both in our respective duties for Jerry, and socially as friends. I admired his abilities, talents, and devotion to Jerry over the years.

Joe and Jerry below in the galley of *Pussycat*.

Jerry's hectic, demanding schedule didn't leave him as much time onboard as he wanted, but he flew in on weekends as often as possible. I picked him up at the airport with a car he kept at the marina for our use. Lincoln Motors gave him a new car every year "for advertising purposes," which came in very handy.

Patti and Joe in the galley of *Pussycat*.

I was greatly impressed by some of the guests Jerry brought aboard – famous people we all knew from the entertainment world, including John Wayne, Tyrone Power, Frank Sinatra, Peter Lawford, Sammy Davis, Jr., Ronald Reagan, and Marilyn Monroe. Presidents John F. Kennedy and Jimmy Carter came, too. Too bad I didn't have a cell phone! I couldn't very well walk into the salon and snap a Polaroid picture, which was the camera of choice in those days. And, YES, Marilyn was a real LOOKER!

Jerry, Joe, and Joe Stabile in a moment of mirth.

Early in 1965, Jerry wanted a bigger boat. He traded in *Pussycat* and decided to buy a new 65-foot Chris Craft Motor Yacht, which he also called *Pussycat*. I went to the dealer in Florida and laid out the equipment for the new vessel, including two big V-12 engines. I knew Jerry liked to go fast, and these would give him the necessary power.

Pussycat.

The order was submitted and soon after I flew to Pompano Beach to oversee the last few weeks of refitting, and go on the sea trials. We took delivery in September of 1965, and I prepared for the trip to San Diego by hiring the crew: Mac Campbell, engineer, Stuart Glennon, mate, and Frank Chapman, cook and deckhand. With all hands and supplies aboard, we set out for Nassau in the Bahamas on the first leg of our journey.

The next day we left for the island of Great Inagua, then on to Port Royal. After 52 hours, we arrived at the Panama Canal. We dropped the anchor in the Quarantine Zone and hoisted the yellow quarantine flag. In due time the inspector arrived to check out our papers and see if there was any illness on board. He gave permission to proceed, and we hired the required pilot to navigate us through the canal.

The coast of Costa Rica was the most beautiful. Jerry didn't go on the trip. He was too busy making money to support my lifestyle!

Pussycat.

Jerry's new 65-foot Chris Craft *Pussycat* at her Kona Kai slip on Shelter Island in San Diego Bay. *Pussycat* is sporting new paint, carpet, furniture, additional electronics, and many more upgrades. She looked first class, sparkling, and ready to go! She had a salon, three staterooms, three heads (bathrooms), a galley, and crew's quarters for me and my assistant.

In early July 1966, Jerry had a show to do in San Francisco, so he said, "Joe, bring the boat to the St. Francis Yacht Club – I'll see you later on." I hired my old shipmate Stuart Glennon to serve as crew. Jerry couldn't spare the time to go on trips during that period, due to a full schedule of movie-making and personal appearances, but he wanted to enjoy his new *Pussycat* during breaks in his San Francisco show.

We had an uneventful trip to San Francisco. On the weekends, Jerry invited members of the cast and friends to take cruises on the bay and see Alcatraz and Pier 66, and to enjoy the sights of San Francisco. Then it was back to the show.

The day before we were scheduled to return to San Diego, Jerry surprised me by saying he'd like to make the trip to San Diego with me. I was pleased that he took the time to enjoy his boat. We left late afternoon. Aboard were Hal Bell who worked as one of Jerry's film directors, Carol Saraceno, Jerry's secretary, Glennon, and myself. We made one stop in Monterey for a late dinner and then headed for San Diego.

The weather was bad – fog and rough seas. An hour or two after Monterey, the high water alarm went off. I went to the engine room to check it out and, sure enough, water was pouring in under the port engine. The pumps couldn't keep up with the incoming water. I pulled a mattress off one of the beds and tried to stuff it under the engine to slow the water, but it didn't help much. I then put in a May Day call to the Coast Guard and gave them our position (and said lots of prayers). We were about five miles off the coast at the time. I could see no hope of saving the boat, so we headed for shore. I could hear the Coast Guard airplane overhead, but it couldn't see us in the fog. The water was coming in fast and soon the engines quit. We dropped anchor about a mile offshore. I inflated the life raft and had everyone put on life jackets and get into the raft. I grabbed a sack of toys I had bought my kids in San Francisco and we set off for shore. The boat anchor couldn't hold the yacht in place, so the boat was drifting toward shore.

Jerry asked me if I had put his briefcase onboard the raft, and I said, "No, I didn't see it." I found out later that he had several thousand dollars and jewelry in the briefcase – I wonder if a lucky diver ever found it?

The boat was breaking up by now. It was a sorry sight as the waves tore it to pieces. We did okay in the raft, up to about 300 yards offshore, but then the waves capsized the raft and we all ended up in the cold water. We were very lucky to land exactly where we did. The coastline in that area is mostly sheer cliffs, and if we had been a mile in either direction, we would surely have been killed – the heavy surf and cliffs would have spelled our doom. A couple of fishermen on the beach had two cars, and they gave us a lift to the Coast Guard Station to report that we were safe.

Jerry Lewis Safe As Yacht Sinks

Comedian Jerry Lewis' $350,000 luxury yacht Pussycat, en route to the Kona Kai Club from San Francisco, sprang a leak a mile off the coast south of Monterey early yesterday and broke up on the rocky shore.

Lewis, his secretary and three men escaped in a rubber life raft, which was overturned by a large wave at the surf line, forcing them to swim the last 30 yards to shore.

No one was hurt.

The yacht has been based at the Kona Kai since March. It was due to arrive here yesterday.

PLANK SPRUNG

R. Martin Hansen, dock master at Kona Kai, said a plank on the port side of the 65-foot cabin cruiser "sprang open, flooding the engine." Water poured into the craft too fast for its pumps to handle.

Lewis, his secretary, Carol Saraceno, crewmen Joe Proux and Art Glennon and Lewis' assistant director, Hal Bell, grabbed life jackets and jumped into a rubber raft after dropping anchor a mile offshore in 60 feet of water and lighting flares.

The Coast Guard said the sinking craft broke loose from its anchor and crashed against the rocks. "It was a total loss," a Coast Guard spokesman said.

FINISHED SHOW

After Lewis and his party made their way through the surf, they were taken to a cafe near San Simeon where they were given coffee and blankets. Later they were taken to Morro Bay, where Lewis telephoned to Los Angeles for an automobile.

Lewis completed a week's engagement at the San Carlos Circle Theater on the peninsula Sunday.

He had purchased the yacht for $200,000 last January and had just completed installing $150,000 in electronics equipment and furniture. A spokesman said the comedian had planned to take his wife, Patti, and five of their six children on a trip to Acapulco within two weeks.

Hansen said Lewis was "mighty proud of that boat. He had it fixed up to perfection and it was beautiful." The dock master said the motor yacht had two V-12 engines of 540 horsepower each and had a maximum speed of 25 knots.

—United Press International Telephoto

ALL THAT'S LEFT OF THE PUSSYCAT

Splintered remains of 65-foot yacht Pussycat lie in surf off coast of Northern California near San Simeon. Comedian Jerry Lewis, the owner, and four others aboard abandoned the $250,000 craft after it started taking on water faster than pumps could keep it afloat. No one was injured.

This was one of the very rare times that Jerry had no jokes or antics. He was a very sober, but grateful man. It was a sad return to San Diego and an empty dock, except for the 18-foot *Bellboy*, Jerry's original runabout. He asked if I would stay on to take care of it, and I said, "Doing what?" So we agreed that I should find other work and he wrote me the following letter of recommendation. I went to work as Captain of the Lockheed Aircraft boat which was used as a selling platform for airplane prospects. The company was selling the Lockheed L1011 plane at that time.

RRY LEWIS PRODUCTIONS INC.*

COLUMBIA STUDIOS
1438 GOWER STREET
HOLLYWOOD, CALIF. 90028
TELEPHONE: 469-8211
CABLE: "LAFFILM"

October 4, 1966

To whom it may concern:

This will advise that Joe Proulx was in my employ from October 13, 1963 through August 27, 1966.

During that time he served as my skipper in charge of my original yacht, the 42 ft. twin engine gasoline cabin cruiser, "Pussycat," and later my 65 ft. twin diesel motor yacht, "Pussycat."

His workmanship was of the highest quality, and his knowledge of the sea is unquestionable. Aside from handling the petty cash, he personally handled many of the purchases made for both vessels.

While Mr. Proulx was in my employ I found him to be dependable, reliable, loyal, and his honesty is beyond reproach. Undoubtedly, he would still be in my employ if the vessel had not been lost at sea on July 19, 1966.

Jerry Lewis

JL/c

* FILMS FOR FUN

TIME FOR ANOTHER BOAT—AND MY RETURN

2

In 1968, Jerry bought a 77-foot Broward that he named *Pussycat Too*. It was located in Florida and Jerry asked me to come back and work for him. Once again, I flew east to bring the yacht through the Panama Canal.

As I joined the crew getting her ready for the trip, I noticed that each day at noon, this fellow joined the guys for lunch. He was always right on time waiting for his handout – a sandwich the guys threw to him – fun for him to appear as if on command.

Our regular lunch guest.

Excerpt of my ship's log

LOG OF YACHT_____

DATE __3-5-68__   PORT __NASSAU N.P.__ TO __GREAT INAGUA__

Departure	Time	LOG of REVS.	CHART COURSE	COURSE STEERED	Wind	Bar.	Therm.	REMARKS
10:30		1800	114°	114°	2	30.01	78°	TO BEACON CAY LIGHT ACROSS YELLOW BANK — SEA DEAD CALM
1400 HRS.		1800	114°		3	30.00	80°	ABEAM BEACON CAY LIGHT CHANGE COURSE TO 135°
1400 HRS		1800	132°	135°	5	30.02	80°	COURSE CHANGE NEXT LIGHT CAPE ST. MARIA SEA CALM
2210		1800	132°	135°	12	30.00	74°	DEVILS POINT LIGHT 12 MI OFF PORT BEAM
0220 (3-6-68)		1800	148°	151°	2	30.00	73°	CAPE ST. MARIA LIGHT CHANGE COURSE TO 151° SEA CALM
0510		1800	148°	151°	0	30.00	73°	CLARENCE TOWN LIGHT 6 MI OFF S. BEAM SUN JUST COMMING OVER HORIZON
0610		1800	157°	160°	5	30.00	72°	CHANGE COURSE TO 160° FOR CASTLE ISLAND SLIGHT GROUND SWELL
0800								STOPPED ENGINES TO CHECK OIL — ADD 4 QTS PORT 5 QTS STAR START FUEL TRANSFER FROM FWD TANK TO MAIN — FINISH 0900 NEXT COURSE CHANGE CASTLE ISLAND. MANY SHIPS IN AREA
12:30		1800	157°	160°	20	29.90	84°	ROUND CASTLE ISLAND LIGHT TURN TO 157° NEXT STOP MATHENTON GREAT INAGUA

26 TOTAL HOURS THIS PAGE

DANFORTH WHITE YACHT LOG

Pussycat Too going through the Panama Canal.

Excerpt of my ship's log

LOG OF YACHT

DATE 7.16.69   PORT BALBOA PANAMA TO GOLFITO, COSTA RICA

Departure	Time	LOG of REVS.	CHART COURSE	COURSE STEERED	Wind	Bar.	Therm.	REMARKS
1430		1800				29.72	90°	
1450		1800	196°	193°	05	29.72	90°	70 MI. TO CAPE MALA
2145		1800	196°	193	15	29.88	79°	OFF CAPE MALA 11 KNOTS
2400		1800	240°	237°	5	29.85	79°	TURNED TO 237° TO 0315 HRS
0315		1800	274°	270°	14	29.85	80°	70 ISLA JICARITA
1200		1800	305	302°	55E	29.85	82°	TO GOLFITO, COSTA RICA
1800		1800	309°	306°	12 SE	29.67	78°	" " "
0150						29.83	81°	SHUT DOWN GOLFITO, COSTA RICA TOOK ON 665 GALS FUEL.
1530		1800			16	29.75	90°	LEFT GOLFITO ✶ ✶ FOR LA UNION COAST OF COSTA RICA IS MOST BEAUTIFUL
1900		1800	292°	297°		29.15	89°	TO CABO BLANCO - LIGHT
0430		1800	292°	297°	-10	29.81	88°	OF CABO BLANCO - LIGHT NOT OPERATING.
ALL DAY		1800	292°	297°	TO 50	29.81	90°	GULF OF PAPAGAYO - BAD DAY HEAVY SEA ON STAR. BOW. MANY LEAKS! COMPRESSOR CAUGHT FIRE. HAD TO TURN OFF ELECTRICITY TWO PART OF BOAT. MAC SAVED THE DAY.
0200		1800	312°	308°	TO 40	29.83	80°	ROLLICOASTER ALL NIGHT - CAN SEE ACTIVE VOLCANOS ON THE BEACH (6 MI.)
0950			ENTRANCE TO GULF OF FONSECA -					ARMY BRIG. GENERAL ON BOARD FOR PAPERS - DUE TO TROUBLE WITH GUATEMALA
1100			SHUT DOWN IN HARBOR TEMP 102° GOT FUEL 715 GAL. CLEARANCE					

69:30 HRS.

DANFORTH WHITE YACHT LOG

Pussycat Too going through the Panama Canal.

Pussycat Too Haulout and Repair.

Pussycat Too at Kona Kai dock, San Diego.

Joe at Kona Kai Club dock in San Diego.

Patti and Joe at Kona Kai Club
dock aboard *Pussycat Too*.

One day Jerry asked me to bring some items to him at his home. I drove up to Bel Air and a private security cop stopped me at the front gate to check my identification. He had been hired to do crowd control, and keep tourists on the bus tours from approaching the house.

I ran into this fellow again when Jerry invited me to his movie set at Paramount Studios to watch the filming. People were standing around the stage area, and Jerry and my "cop" friend were engaged in a very heated argument. Jerry hauled off and hit him in the face, the cop fell down, immediately pulled his gun, and shot Jerry twice. Everyone was in shock as Jerry fell to the floor. Then they got up and hugged each other! Anything for a laugh!

Humor was the running theme with Jerry, both professionally and in his everyday life. He was very spontaneous, and could come up with a funny prank or story at will. He sent me an example of a joke involving comedian Jack Benny, who had a reputation of being a tightwad. In fact, Jack was a very generous man.

PLAYING GOLF WAS NOT AS MUCH FUN AS BEATING HIM FOR THE
DOLLAR.....THIS IS HOW HE PAID.
IN NOV.1950.

LOVE,

JERRY

When my son Larry broke his arm, Jerry created and sent him this get-well message.

Pussycat Too at the Kona Kai dock, San Diego.

From 1968 through the late 1970s, Jerry continued to enjoy his yacht *Pussycat Too*. We took her to Catalina and Newport Beach, CA, and he often came down for weekends. Sadly, as the time went on, his schedule took him out of town often, and his marriage to Patti ended in divorce. My marriage also ended. So many changes took place during those years. Jerry finally sold *Pussycat Too* and I went to work for other yacht owners.

Jerry remarried in 1983, and in 1989 he and his wife, Sam, chartered a yacht and came to San Diego to meet their broker, Neil Dreischmeyer. Neil had acted as Jerry's broker in former yacht purchases, and now suggested a 1961 Grebe, a 75-foot classic wooden yacht, needing some tender, loving care. With the necessary upgrades, it could become one of the shining stars of San Diego Bay. Jerry and Sam were excited about the prospects of having a "haven" when Jerry's packed schedule allowed for some rest and relaxation. The potential of this fine vessel gave them a reason to call on me once again, to help make their dreams come true.

I had been working in San Diego for various yacht owners and hiring crews to remodel, when Jerry stopped by to offer me a new position. It was a challenging opportunity, and I eagerly accepted his offer. So began a 12-year unique relationship with Jerry, including many more social occasions, and the development of a personal friendship among Jerry, Sam, me and Shirley, my new wife of 9 years. It was an extremely fulfilling time for all of us.

Neil Dreischmeyer, Sam and Jerry.

Jerry was a genius, in my opinion, especially in his ability to make people laugh. After an evening out with him, we returned home with stomachs sore from the bellylaughs we enjoyed. He was spontaneous, and had an instant, comic response to almost every situation. I often envied his ability to act out his reactions – much as we would like to, but didn't have the courage. He was kind and generous – he never left us out of the loop. We shared many wonderful dinners and unique opportunities, seeing and joining in special airings or shows and events. He often asked me to print various items for him, creating some much-needed business for my commercial printing company. Jerry's favorite color was red, so we used a lot of fire-engine red ink during that time!

One night he took Joe and me to the Russian circus. We trailed along while he spoke to the performers as they prepared for the show. We came to the trainer of a VERY large brown bear and, to my amazement, Jerry walked over and gave the bear a big hug! I never knew if that had been pre-arranged or he just felt like doing it. Even the bear looked surprised! If only I'd had my camera.

I noticed on several occasions he turned down autograph seekers, and I asked him why? He said we were in an area where it was possible to create a stampede of folks all wanting to get in on the action, and it could be dangerous. I had never thought of that. He was often the object of public interest and usually it was a mutually-enjoyable event. I did see on several occasions how rude and demanding some people were, asking for autographs and pictures. Often he left unfinished meals rather than create a scene. Being a celebrity was not all it was cracked up to be.

Once a particularly obnoxious man and his wife insisted that Sam take a picture of them with Jerry. Sam sweetly complied and handed the camera back to the happy departing couple. We said, "That was really nice of you – they were awful!" Sam replied with a smile, "Wait until they develop them – I cut off their heads!"

~SHIRLEY

As captain, I had to follow new environmental protection laws that required most remodeling and painting of yachts take place in a "controlled" area – no more fouling of the bay with trash. We took *Sam's Place* to South Bay Boat Yard, where the painting and re-enforcing of the hull took place. They had the equipment to move a 68-ton boat like it was a toy. The final result was a vessel that was safe, sound, and sparkling with her new paint job. The necessary mechanical repairs were also done while she was on the rail track ways.

We brought her back to her new home, the Marriott Marina, affording every convenience the Lewis family wanted, and set against the beautiful backdrop of San Diego Bay and Skyline. I went to work remodeling the interior of the salon and staterooms, which were dated and in need of beautification. Sam jumped in with much enthusiasm, picking out colors, textures, and patterns, along with furnishings that created a comfortable and very attractive home. She was given complete freedom (after all, the yacht was named after her!), as long as she featured Jerry's favorite color – fire-engine red! The carpet, galley décor, master stateroom – even the runabout *Jerry's Place* – were bright, bright red! It turned out to be breath-taking!.

Sam's Place on the Ways.

Sam's Place in repair.

The hull repair—a mahogany insert.

Sam's Place sparkling and beautiful, heading for the Marriott dock.

Sam's Place, the yacht.

Jerrys Place, the runabout.

Jerry enjoying his birthday gift.

Sam asked me to have a great big red bow placed around Jerry's birthday chair when he came aboard. He was surprised and thrilled, and immediately put it to good use.

Each time Jerry came to *Sam's Place*, we enjoyed watching him "unwind." You could see the years and tension fall away as he eased into his chair, turned on the TV, and put the recliner into position – a big smile came over his face – Heaven!

Sam is going after the Big One.

Expert advice helps.

Success!

Warm congratulations!

HAPPENINGS

The award for Special Achievement in Yacht Restoration is unique. It takes a special kind of person to look into the heart of a lady who has been down on her luck for a number of years and make the commitment to restore her to her former glory. It is not a job for the faint of heart. It takes patience, skill, determination and some major bucks.

This year's award goes to "Sam's Place", owned by Sam and Jerry Lewis (yes, *that* Jerry Lewis). Special congratulations also go to her Captain, Master Mariner, Master Carpenter and Shipwright, Good Guy Extraordinaire, Joe Proulx.

A portion of the Marina newsletter, 1991

1991

SPECIAL ACHIEVEMENT
IN YACHT RESTORATION

AWARDED TO

M.Y. "Sam's Place"

Jerry and Sam Lewis

Owners

Joe Proulx, Captain

San Diego Marriott

Marina

AN INVITATION

Shortly after Joe began his beautification project on Sam's Place, Jerry and Sam invited us to Las Vegas to see Jerry appear with Sammy Davis, Jr. It was a wonderful show, and the team of Lewis and Davis was fantastic. After the show, we were invited backstage to visit the Lewises and share a glass of champagne. Angel, their adorable Shih Tzu, sat next to Sam on the couch sharing her attention.

Sammy walked in and he was very friendly as we were introduced. What a thrill to meet him in person and be able to compliment him on his fine performance. He was a very special friend of Jerry, and they enjoyed a close relationship, both professionally and personally. Sammy explained that he had performed while he was in great pain from his hip. He covered it well and danced as if nothing were wrong. Later we found out he was on heavy doses of pain medication to enable him to go "on" as planned. "Troopers" seem to have the almost superhuman ability to hide personal suffering and pain – we saw that ability with Jerry many times, as he battled various ailments and problems. Jerry and Sammy were very committed to their craft, and we were lucky to have witnessed their talent that night.

We were also invited to visit the Lewises at their home in Las Vegas. My first time there we got the grand tour – a most impressive brick mansion, with beautiful décor and many accolades and mementos of Jerry's work through the years. I was impressed that all the scripts from his movies were beautifully bound in signature red leather books with gold embossed titles and displayed in handsome bookshelves along an upper gallery. I couldn't believe how many there were – very impressive!

As usual, that first visit was full of laughter – what else would you expect from a host like Jerry Lewis?

~SHIRLEY

A warm welcome to the Lewis home in Las Vegas,
Sam, Joe, and Joe Stabile, Jerry's manager.

Cocktails with the pet Shih Tzus, Joe, Shirley, and Jerry at the Lewis home.

Joe, Shirley, and Angel.

A MIRACLE 5 OCCURS

We feel blessed to have been able to share a miracle in the Lewises' lives. Sam had so longed for a child and unfortunately had not been able to have a successful pregnancy. The disappointment was a sad time for them both and difficult to accept.

Late in 1991, their miracle happened – adopting a baby who was due in March of 1992. This called for major planning and whipping out the knitting needles and patterns that would enhance the new arrival's layette. I was so thrilled to be included in the plans – I had not yet had the joy of becoming a grandmother, so this was a happy experience – something to be savored and enjoyed.

Sam and I added to our creative skills by taking classes in smocking – a beautiful, old needlecraft that yielded adorable baby clothes. Sam was very adept and worked hard to make them "special" to suit the new arrival. She found a woman to give her a lesson in smocking, and spent many hours on the set of Jerry's film in New Mexico, working on the baby's clothes. I was back in San Diego smocking. Sometimes we talked on the phone, and caught up on our news.

Finally, on March 23ʳᵈ a baby girl arrived to complete the family that Sam and Jerry had longed for. She was named Danielle Sarah, after Jerry's father and grandmother. Jerry had six sons from his previous marriage to Patti, but this baby girl was a new experience that totally enthralled him. Sam took to motherhood like a champ with all its demands, worries, and joys. We awaited the exciting day she would return to Sam's Place and we could hold her in our arms.

Ever the practical one, Joe began to plan and execute the changes that were necessary to make the yacht "baby-proof." He installed gates, locks, and a baby swing on the aft deck for her fun and pleasure.

~SHIRLEY

Jerry Ferris

DEAR SHIRLEY;

IT WAS SO GOOD SPEAKING WITH YOU THE OTHER DAY....IT

MADE ME PLENTY HOME SICK FOR "SAM'S PLACE" AND YOU AND

"BIG JOE"...

I HOPE YOU'RE BOTH WELL AND HAPPY.

<u>SAM AND "DANI" AND I CAN'T WAIT !!!!!!!!</u>

IT WONT BE LONG NOW..AND WE'LL BE TOGETHER....

I CAN'T WAIT FOR YOU TO MEET "DANI" SHE WILL MELT YOUR

HEART AS SHE MELTS MINE EVERY MINUTE OF EVERY DAY...

I AM SO SMITTEN I CAN'T SEE STRAIGHT....

BUT YOU'LL SEE THAT....AS WELL AS "SAM'S" FACE...SHE'S

A TOTALLY DIFFERENT WOMAN....THE PEACE AND SERENITY ON

HER FACE MAKES YOU WANT TO JUMP UP AND DOWN FOR JOY

SEEING SOMEONE COME AROUND LIKE THAT...

WELL YOU'LL SEE.....

ON SUNDAY OR MONDAY....

ALL OUR LOVE...

ALWAYS,

JERRY

7/22/92

FED/EX/

Danielle arrives home in Las Vegas.

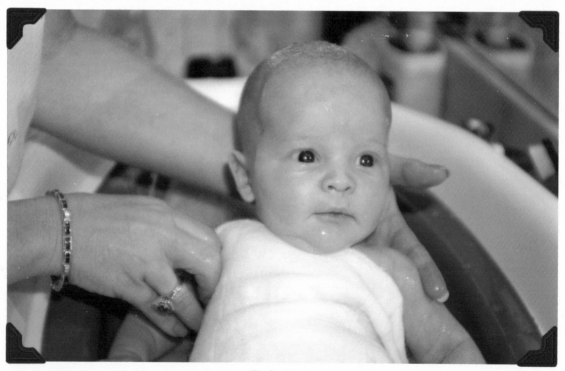

Bath time.

Dani's first trip to *Sam's Place*, 1992.

Dani in Shirley's arms.

Shirley and Dani, aboard *Sam's Place* at the Marriott Marina, San Diego Bay.

Our smocked gift for Dani.

Dear Shirley & Joe —
We really don't know how to thank you enough for such a precious piece of art work. It's expression touches our hearts. It will truly be treasured. Thank you for your wonderful friendship. We love you —
Sam & Jerry

A thank-you note from Sam and Jerry.

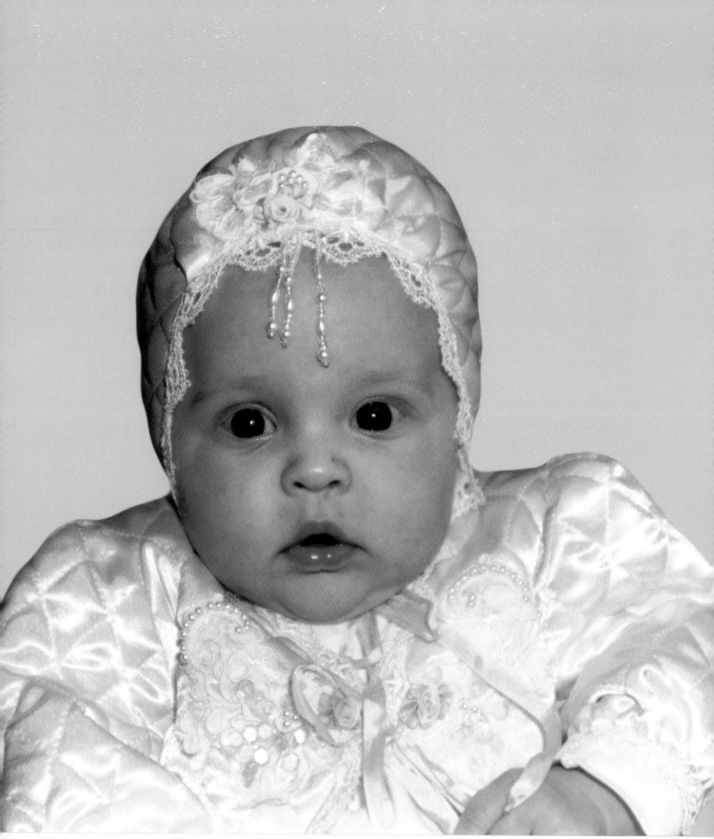

Dani in a lovely pearl-encrusted dress and cap.

Jerry clowning with Dani's teething ring.

Jerry presenting friend Rudi with a birthday bouquet (weeds)
at Morton's Steakhouse in downtown San Diego.

Sam, Dani, and Jerry.

The proud parents.

Dear Friends and Family,

In June, I graduated from Kindergarten with a very good report card. Because my report card was so good, Mommy and Daddy bought me a new Shih Tzu puppy. My puppy is chocolate, with black tips, and her name is "Jolie." Last year, some girls in my class and I took a Ballet, Tap, and Jazz combo class, and in June, we performed in our first recital to the song, "You Musta Been a Beautiful Baby."

During the summer, my friend Nicole was here visiting me from Florida. We had so much fun together. We went to the movies, Wet-N-Wild, and played in my backyard and pool. We also played miniature golf, and I got a HOLE IN ONE! We even made up a dance routine to "GREASE!" "Grease" is my favorite movie right now, and my favorite character is "Sandy."

The end of my summer Mommy, Daddy, "Jolie," and I went to San Diego to spend some time on our boat. We had a lot of fun and it was nice to get out of the Vegas heat and go to the San Diego breeze.

I started First Grade at the end of August. The enclosed pictures were Daddy's surprise Father's Day gift from mommy and me. I hope you like them!

Love,

Danielle Sara

Rudi gives Dani a "swing" on the aft deck.

Proud Papa and Dani onboard *Sam's Place*.

First time in the snow – cold!

Hamming it up! Where does she get that?

Dani's mom dressed her adorably. We especially loved her hats and the fact she left them on!

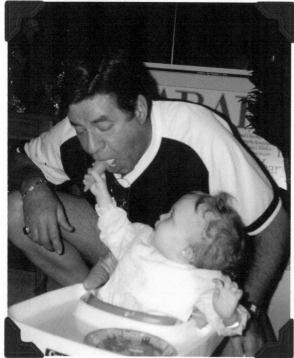

Dani is growing up.

Sam and Dani.

Ready to explore her nautical world with Mom.

GUESS WHO'S COMING TO DINNER?

Several times the Lewises came to our Point Loma home for dinner. These were special evenings for us – Jerry, of course, kept us entertained and laughing throughout, and Sam was the gracious, supportive lady to his clowning, as always.

One memorable evening they came to welcome our new Bishon puppy, P-Nutte. She was a tiny bundle of joy whom we had brought home just a few days earlier. They came with a baby puppy-size boat bed – fire-engine red, of course, and lots of toys to go with it.

It was such a kind gesture on their part, and we were again touched by their thoughtfulness.

~SHIRLEY

P-Nutte and Jerry share a snuggle.

P-Nutte's new boat bed.

Dani meets P-Nutte.

More hugs for P-Nutte from Sam.

Our birthday gift to Sam was a hand-made smocked nightgown, and her cake was decorated the same – smocked! We just had to celebrate our fun, learning the craft together.

Sam and Jerry.

Many happy returns, Sam!

Jerry's ON!

Joe, Shirley, Mary Lou, Scott (Jerry's son), Jerry, and Sam.

THE TELETHON TRIPS

One of the most rewarding benefits of Joe's years with Jerry was our invitations to attend the Muscular Dystrophy Association Telethon. We had watched the show on TV many times, but to see it in person was a different experience. During the 22-hour plea for funds to benefit "Jerry's Kids," we were allowed to watch the "total" event: rehearsals with famous stars, visits with many of the children and their families featured on the show, and the enjoyable music of a 36-piece orchestra. As Jerry went through an amazing effort to raise more money every year, our trips were a once-in-a-lifetime event, and we enjoyed participating several times – both in Las Vegas and then in Hollywood at the CBS studios. We were treated like visiting royalty.

~ SHIRLEY

Joe and Shirley onstage at the Telethon.

Our beautiful hotel.

Our MDA badge.

Rehearsal time, Joe and Jerry.

Joe, Shirley and Joey attend a Telethon rehearsal.

A laugh (again) at rehearsal.

Dani's first Telethon with proud Mom.

Shirley, Joe, and friends enjoy a rehearsal.

Jerry clowns with Barbershop Singers - hilarious!

Jerry checks the TV monitor.

Jerry rehearses with singer Charo.

Charo was a favorite of adults and children alike.

She was a very talented and friendly lady. Here she and Dani talk to a stagehand.

Eddie Foy, Jr. and Joe.

Jerry and his support staff.

Rudi, Joe, and Jerry before the Telethon began.

Dress Rehearsal with Shirley and Joe in the foreground.

Jerry performs with Jann Carl,
a long-time friend of MDA.

Jann served as Telethon
National Co-Host in 1996.

Jann was beautiful, charming,
and very talented.

Jann also served as
National Board of
Director and National
Vice President of MDA.

During the Telethon trips, we saw first-hand the many-faceted Jerry Lewis – and the application of his craft and talent. It was an opportunity to see his technical expertise and how he noted every detail of the production. His unflagging energy was amazing.

During the 1997 Telethon, Jerry faced a unforeseen emergency. Princess Diana's death was announced. It shocked the entire world – and could have thrown the Telethon into chaos. Indeed it was a major personal crisis for Jerry and Sam, who had met Diana while they were in London for Jerry's appearance in "Damn Yankees." They had talked about future plans for her participation in benefits for her various causes. She was warm and welcoming, and they liked her immensely. Now, to reflect the correct manner of sorrow and respect during the airing of the Telethon, was an almost impossible effort, but Jerry did it. We were amazed at the appropriate changes to the schedule and of the show – especially the early part where Jerry addressed the situation with love and sorrow – speaking for all of us who couldn't believe such an event could happen.

Never was he "taller" in our opinion. It was a beautiful honoring of a beloved person and done almost instantly as the airing of the Telethon began. Amazing!

Sam, Dani, and Claudia during a break.

The opportunity to meet the children featured on the show was unique. Joe and I met several of his "Poster Children" in the years we attended, and they were very impressive. They were cursed by the tragedy of neuro-muscular disease, but they were blessed with an extra talent or insight that touched our minds and souls. They were also comfortable with the attention and being "on stage," delightful in their interaction with Jerry, and obviously thrilled with the Telethon experience.

One of our favorites was Mattie Stepanek, a boy with a rare form of muscular dystrophy, and a poet from the age of three. His book Hope Through Heartsongs *we read and enjoyed. It was filled with insights and a unique way of envisioning life and beyond that was unearthly. His insights transcend time as we knew it, and you had only to see him briefly to feel his "specialness." In his too-short life, he left us with beautiful memories, as well as his poetry to hold him in our hearts.*

~ SHIRLEY

Dani cheers on the Telethon success.

Hugs and congratulations Jerry, from Eddie Foy, Jr.

Jerry's co-host Ed McMahon and more meet backstage after the Telethon ends.

Jerry, Claudia, and guests.

Jerry is exhausted but still standing after 22 and 1/2 hours of the MDA telecast.

Frank Sinatra arranged a "surprise guest" for Jerry at the 1976 Telethon!

Joe always had *Sam's Place* decorated to celebrate a very
successful Telethon, and to welcome Jerry home.

45 million dollars was the amount raised. When Jerry saw the sign
"$45 million," he said "You'll never get that much for the boat!"

 MDA CAMP

Jerry and I traveled up to the Cuyamaca Mountains east of San Diego to support and encourage the kids attending summer camp. He made many guest appearances on behalf of MDA throughout the year all over the country. This was a hot summer day and after talking with the kids for several hours, he went to a local store and bought them all ice cream! It was a typical, Jerry-like loving gesture to bring joy to the kids.

Jerry entertains the camp children.

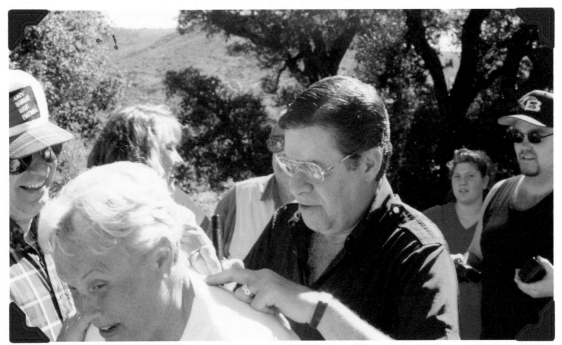

Jerry gives an autograph to a fan.

Jerry tells jokes to a gathering of kids.

REMODELING THE AFT DECK
9

In 1995, while Jerry was in New York and London appearing in "Damn Yankees," I began the beautification and upgrades of the aft deck on *Sam's Place*. All construction projects begin with moving all the "stuff" and a happy attitude!

"Stuff."

A happy attitude.

The old construction consisted of canvas and plastic side curtains. The aft enclosure was the same materials with a zippered closure. The overhead was perforated cloth. As you can see in the pictures, I built angled supports of mahogany on about a 15-degree angle. These had sliding tracks, so the glass could be opened or closed. The new aft enclosure was also done in mahogany with a sliding door.

I tore out the ugly overhead and replaced it with tongue and groove 1 x 4 spruce, with mahogany trim to dress it up.

Jerry enjoyed spending time writing and reading on the aft deck, so I made a coffee-type table that raised and lowered with a push of a button. The table could also slide forward or away from you. An end table on both sides of a curved settee finished off that area.

Cabinets at the forward end enclosed a washer, dryer, and small refrigerator.
During construction I wired in overhead lights and side-mounted lamps.

Project Completed!

Jerry Lewis

JAN.19.1995

DEAR JOE;

WE LEAVE ON SAT.JAN.28TH.
WE SURE ARE GONNA MISS YOU AND SHIRLEY AND "SAM'S PLACE"
MAYBE YOU,AND SHIRLEY MIGHT THINK ABOUT A TRAIN RIDE TO
NEW YORK CITY SOME WEEKEND AND SEE THE SHOW ? ? ?
PLEASE KEEP IN TOUCH AND LET ME KNOW...
WE CAN MAKE THE ARRANGEMENTS FOR HOUSING AND THE SHOW
IF YOU LET US KNOW WITH SOME LEAD TIME.

ENCLOSED FIND CHECKS...NOTE THE DATE AND EACH MONTH
ON THE FIRST I WILL GET THEM OUT TO YOU..

WATCH OUR "BOAT" AND CARE FOR ONE ANOTHER UNTIL WE CAN
ALL BE TOGETHER AGAIN...

WE SEND YOU ALL OUR LOVE..

GIVE RUDY OUR BEST AND IF NEW YORK WORKS OUT MAYBE HE'LL
JOIN YOU GUYS...JUST LET US KNOW..

LOVE AND TALK TO YOU BEFORE THE 28TH

"QUEEG"

P.S. SHIRLEY MILLER SAID THE AFT DECK IS TO DIE FROM
     SHE THINKS IT'S MADE THE BOAT...

LOVE

Joe

love To you
and Shirley

I'm having the
Time of my Life —

love + xxx

Julie

You, Shirley + Rudi Must Come!

Sam + Danii Send love —

Who wouldn't be thrilled to receive such exciting invitations to see Jerry on Broadway?

Preparing to leave town for a couple of weeks was not an easy task. We arranged for boat-sitters, printing-company sitters, house-sitters, and pet-sitters. Joe had put the finishing touches on his remodeling of the aft deck, so he was ready for a vacation. Our friend, Rudi Enners planned to join us in New York, and we knew that he would add greatly to our fun and enjoyment with his wonderful sense of humor and enthusiasm.

For Joe, who had never visited New York, it was the trip of a lifetime. We were able to get reservations on Amtrak in June 1995. I'm a terrified non-flyer, so we had the bonus of seeing the good old USA from the train. It was a year of floods through the Mid-West, and many passengers embarking in Kansas were full of stories that tore at our hearts: loss of crops, property damage, and other calamities. It was like living a front-page newspaper story and had a reality that hit home with us. The train even had to be delayed for a period because of the tracks being under water.

We heard interesting lectures about areas we passed through. Our private compartment came with a charming steward who saw that we never lacked for wine, cheese, and crackers at Happy Hour – bless him. It was challenging to balance in our private, but oh-so-tiny shower stall as the train rocked along at high speed – especially after Happy Hour!

We had a layover in Chicago for a tour of the beautiful lakefront and then headed for New York. The trail paralleled the Hudson River and passed the U.S. Army Academy at West Point. Three days after we left San Diego, we arrived in the Big Apple.

~ SHIRLEY

No need to ask us twice, Cap'n Queeg!
We're on our way to see you on Broadway.

New York

We depart June 2, 1995 and arrive
in New York three days later.

Through the years, when we've visited Jerry's sets, dressing rooms, and hotels, we've observed his unique ability to turn any space into a "home away from home." New York's Waldorf Astoria was no exception.

Can you imagine Jerry Lewis in a complete office with all the technical and business equipment he uses, along with Sam, a busy toddler, and her wardrobe, equipment, and toys, and two dogs with their fenced-in play area and bathroom? Jerry was working away and she welcomed us into their temporary "digs" with such warm and happy hugs. How amazing was that?

They stayed in their elegant suite during his New York run of "Damn Yankees." They made the transition look so easy and effortless, but they also had lots of support from their staff. Jerry had been doing these transitions most of his life. When Sam, Dani, and dogs joined him, they simply became more creative and made a home within their hotel space that would afford them comfort and privacy.

Sam and pups welcome us to New York.

Jerry pondering a problem.

Busy as usual in his Waldorf "office."

Jerry, Sam, and Dani treat us to lunch at the Bull & Bear in the Waldorf Astoria.

Dani liked the cherries best of all!

MARQUIS
JERRY LEWIS
DAMN YANKEES

ME0606E ORCH   G 110   ADULT
  EVENT CODE   SECTION/BOX ROW   SEAT   All Taxes Incl. if Applicable
$ 67.50 ORCH CENTER   ADM.$ 67.50
PRICE & ALL TAXES INCL.
                NO REFUNDS/NO EXCHANGES
ORCH   DAMN YANKEES
  SECTION/BOX   7.2.2.
CH   1×   MARQUIS THEATRE
  G 110   1535 BROADWAY
  ROW SEAT
MAR401A   TUE JUN 6,1995 8:00PM
28APR95

MEMO

46th and
Broadway
at the
Marquis
Theater

7:30
Box Office

JERRY LEWIS

THE DEVIL MADE HIM DO IT!

BEGINNING FEB 28

JERRY LEWIS

IN

DAMN YANKEES

To Joe and Shirley love Jerry

Give someone a very *Jerry* Christmas now

WITH TICKETS TO
HIS BROADWAY DEBUT!
A SPECIAL LIMITED ENGAGEMENT!

FOR EXACT SEAT LOCATIONS, CALL TICKETMASTER: (212) 307-4100 (24HRS/7 DAYS)
OUTSIDE NY, NJ, CT: (800) 755-4000 • GROUPS: (212) 768-2990/2988

MARQUIS THEATRE BROADWAY & 46TH STREET

Beginning Jan. 1, this "slam-bang smash" (WCBS-TV) will be on hiatus, as the team goes into Spring Training with our new Devil.
Watch for updates about the Feb. 28 season-opener at the only game in town!

We were invited to join Jerry and Sam at the Malcolm Forbes Galleries for a cast dinner. From the time we took a hair-raising taxi trip down Fifth Ave. to 12ᵗʰ St., walked through the fabulous museum, ate a sumptuous dinner, and said our "Good nights," we experienced many memorable "firsts."

Show business people have an unique quality of support and respect for each other, and are very demonstrative in the way they care. It's rather like a family's love for each other, and it was great to be included in such an approving and warm atmosphere. Unfortunately, cameras were not allowed in the Forbes Galleries, so we couldn't take pictures of the gala evening.

The unique and vast collection that Forbes amassed from the time he was a small child, were awesome: some 500 ships and 12,000 toy soldiers, along with priceless Fabergé eggs. Rudi, Joe, and I savored our tour before the dinner, and would certainly recommend it as an important stop for anyone visiting New York.

The next day, Rudi joined us on a tour of the Empire State Building and Central Park with its charming horse-drawn carriages. We had lunch at Tavern on the Green, then explored St. Patrick's Cathedral and World Trade Center (it was still standing then). We also took a cruise by the beautiful, breathtaking Statue of Liberty, and a trip down Wall Street on a double-decker bus, which broke down halfway through the afternoon.

Rudi treated us to a lovely dinner in the revolving restaurant 41 floors above the city at the Marriott Hotel – a beautiful 360-degree view.

The Lewises took us to a Southern feast at Jezebel's Restaurant – delicious! You had to know it was there – there was no sign outside.

After a whirlwind of activity and events, we boarded our train for the journey home. It was a special, wonderful, and unique adventure. Joe remarked, "I was amazed how enjoyable and interesting train travel can be."

~SHIRLEY

Our Welcome-Home Committee

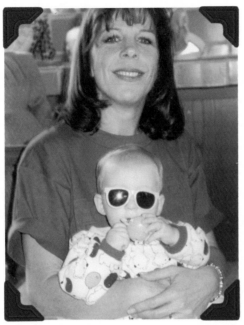

Susan and Jamie, Shirley's daughter and grandson.

P-Nutte and Scooter were very happy to have us home again.

OUR STAR RETURNS

After "Damn Yankees" closed in New York, and before going to London, Jerry and family returned for some needed R & R on *Sam's Place*. We welcomed him, celebrating his huge success in not only New York but various other cities, with a huge "Bravo Applegate" banner – a visual applause to his talent and tremendous effort.

After a short time relaxing on Sam's Place, Jerry and his family traveled to London to perform in "Damn Yankees" until the show closed.

~SHIRLEY

When Jerry brought the show to San Diego, we asked many of our friends to join us for an afternoon of first-rate entertainment. We saw a new level of happiness and satisfaction in Jerry – he was living his dream in this production and having the time of his life! This was what he was born for – to make people laugh and to entertain them. We believe "Damn Yankees" was the highlight of his theatrical career. His father once told him, "You'll be the greatest success when you appear on Broadway."

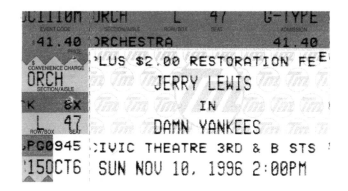

Handwritten on photo: The NIGHT HE HIT "70" 3/16/96

Jerry in his dressing room on his 70th birthday, while he was
performing in "Damn Yankees" in London.

TRIPS TO LAS VEGAS 12

We always looked forward to visiting the Lewises in Las Vegas. Some trips were to lend a hand in a renovation project, some were to attend a show or special event. We always were welcomed with warmth and hugs.

Joe decided to make a model of *Sam's Place* to grace Jerry's home office. To this day, it's Joe's favorite hobby, and this project was a special labor of love. He started with a block of wood – and voila! – ended up with a beautifully-crafted yacht model.

~SHIRLEY

Sam's Place model begins.

Almost ready to launch!

Ready to sail to Las Vegas.

New berth in Jerry's home office.

Jerry hard at work.

Dani with her new puppy Jolie, and Dad.

Jerry's close friends Loretta and Walter Anderson, editor of *Parade Magazine*, and host/manager Joe Stabile at his home in Las Vegas.

Claudia's kitchen (she's hard at work in the background). Jerry planted himself on the center workspace.

Sam, Jerry, and guests enjoy Claudia's superb meal.

Shirley, Jerry, and Joe enjoy an evening at the Stabile's home.

WELCOMING IN A NEW YEAR 13

We enjoyed celebrating the New Year with Jerry and Sam several times. Here are some pictures of our 2000 New Year's Eve celebration aboard *Sam's Place*. The century was changing, and it was the last New Year's Eve we spent with Sam and Jerry. Here is *Sam's Place* all decorated and festive for the big event.

This evening we enjoyed food from the Marriott Hotel, and it was delicious. One New Year's celebration we were treated to peach champagne and caviar – wow! We still remember how special it tasted. Another New Year Jerry took us on a tour of the Bay, ending up under the fireworks! He wanted to get us "really close," and he meant it.

~SHIRLEY

Our 2000 party group on the aft deck – a beautiful setting for a special evening.

Jerry, Dani, and Rudi.

Jerry was consistent over the New Year's Eves we shared. We ate dinner, gathered around the television on the aft deck, and watched the ball drop in Times Square – at 9:00 p.m., California time. Then, with a hug and best wishes, he was off to bed, and we all left after securing the boat.

A FAVORITE DESTINATION—THE CORONADO HOTEL

14

Many weekends Jerry, Sam, Dani, and a multitude of friends set out to enjoy a day on San Diego Bay, journeying an hour to The Coronado Hotel's Crown Room for buffet brunch. Jerry usually "drove," blowing a loud air horn to announce his presence. He was never a quiet person, and entered into any activity with the enthusiasm of a happy, excited kid. His trips to Coronado were a favorite, and we enjoyed it many times with him. He was easily recognized and he jumped in with both feet when a special occasion was celebrated at the hotel. He often appeared in pictures or shared jokes, much to the surprise and delight of all. You never knew what spontaneous antic he'd come up with for a laugh.

~SHIRLEY

All Aboard!

Joe welcomes guests aboard.

Jerry drives full speed ahead.

Sam's Place tied up in Coronado.

Let's eat!

Jerry and Rudi receive admiring smiles from Coronado Hotel guests.

Joe, Deby, Jerry's daughter-in-law, Jerry, Sam, and Shirley in the Crown Room.

The group strolls down Coronado's main street Orange Avenue - Max Alexander, Joe, Shirley, Scott, (Jerry's son,) Jerry, Dani, and Sam.

Captain Joe at the helm.

Ever the clown, Jerry went shopping in a boutique at the Coronado and bought a pillow for the couch on the aft deck. After presenting Sam with her gift and hearing her response ("That's just not going to work, Jerry!"), he gave her one of his famous "looks!"

Don't drink and drive!

Cap'n. Queeg overseeing Joe's work.

Shirley and Jerry share a hug.

Thanks for a perfect day!

End of a lovely day.

TAKE ME OUT TO THE BALLGAME
15

One summer evening Jerry invited Jim Miller and me to join him at a San Diego Padres baseball game. It was great fun. We enjoyed the game in such a unique way, being the guests of a famous star. This was one of the many "perks" we enjoyed during my years with Jerry. Attending shows and events in that manner was a very different experience.

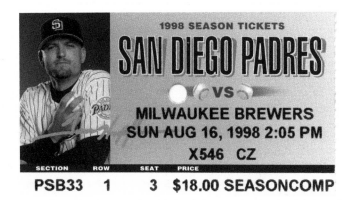

We head for the baseball game - Jerry, Jim, and Joe.

Flanked by Jim and Joe, Jerry prepares to throw out the first pitch.

Jerry Coleman, "Voice of the Padres," Joe and Jim.

Jerry, Joe, and Jim watch the game from the announcer's booth.

Sam, Jerry, Jac Flanders, and Shirley enter Rainwater's Restaurant in San Diego.

Shirley, Joe, and Jerry admire Joe's cake.

Joe receives a piece of his chocolate cake - Shirley, Joe, waiter, and Jerry.

Joe and Jerry pose for the official birthday photo.

Shirley and Joe celebrate the birthday dinner.

Mary Lou and Jac Flanders.

Front - Jerry, Sam, Shirley, Joe, and Jac.
Back - Mary Lou and Sean.

THE RUSSIAN NAVY COMES ABOARD
17

At the end of the Cold War in 1991, the Russians sent two of their warships to San Diego on a goodwill tour. The ships anchored in South Bay, and the U.S. Navy went overboard (just joking) to entertain the Russians.

The U.S.S. Merrill dropped the Russian officers at the Marriott Hotel for a cocktail party and lunch. Later a Navy officer said to me, "These Russians have never been aboard a private yacht. Would you invite them on yours?" "Sure," I said, and welcomed about 20 of them.

I explained that this yacht belonged to Jerry Lewis. One of the Russians said he had seen all of Jerry's films, and was very excited about the tour. When he saw the toilet compartment in the master stateroom, he noted the TV mounted in the wall. His comment was, "Only in America!"

I think a good time was had by all, because the next day I got a call from Navy Commander Bettencourt asking when would Jerry be down on the boat again? I told him that he would be there tomorrow. He gave me a phone number to call – he wanted to set up a tour of the U.S.S. Merrill for Jerry and his group.

Jerry was all for it, so the next day they picked us up and took us to the Navy base in South Bay to board the Merrill – a great day! We toured the ship and had lunch onboard. A few weeks later, I heard Bettencourt was promoted to Captain.

The Russians arrive at the Marriott dock.

The Russians enjoyed their tour of *Sam's Place*.

Commander Bettencourt welcomes us aboard the U.S.S. Merrill.

Commander Bettencourt's official welcoming party.

We enjoyed luncheon onboard the U.S.S. Merrill.

Some of the officers of the U.S.S. Merrill at our luncheon.

HAPPY 74TH JERRY! 18

Sam planned the most elegant party for Jerry's 74th birthday March 16, 2000. She rented the suite at the top of the Hyatt Hotel in San Diego. We were invited to fete Jerry, and enjoy the exquisite décor, cocktails, and a delicious dinner. Every luxury you can imagine was there – ours to enjoy for the evening.

~SHIRLEY

Jerry and Sam set the tone for a happy celebration.

Jerry and Sam seal the evening with a kiss.

As you can see, there were plenty of laughs and gaiety. This beautiful
suite featured a grand piano, and lovely music set off the overall
magnificence of the celebration. Beautiful planning, Sam!

Joe, Shirley, Mary Lou Flanders, Jerry, and Sam (Jac Flanders took the photo).

Sam shows the Chef's "Happy Birthday" creation.

The group enjoyed show tunes by a very talented pianist.

The table was beautifully set. Jerry preferred red wine.

Jerry, Sam, and our waiter.

Time to say "Happy Birthday"
again, and sleep well!

Jerry clowns around with rose petals.

A good deal of my time, as you can see, was spent laughing, eating great food, going to shows and special events, and enjoying the Lewises' company.

In the interest of presenting the "whole" picture, I would like to include some of the notes and correspondence – either just comments or long lists of boat work Jerry wanted me to do to achieve his goals to make his yacht very special. You will notice an underlying comedy which was so much a part of Jerry, and an expression of caring when you read between the lines.

Most of the remodeling and repair took place while Jerry was on the road, giving us the opportunity to create the upset and dirt that went with such projects. There was no pressure during these times, just attention to the job at hand.

The pressure and time constraints came when Jerry and family were due for a visit. This necessitated a trip to the airport to pick him up, sometimes hiring an extra vehicle to help with the luggage, stocking the boat with his favorite foods (and treats – Sam, you didn't read this) and having the boat fueled and immaculate. When the Lewis family was aboard, it was rather like a doctor being "on call." Sometimes I got calls to go down and take care of a plumbing or mechanical problem in the middle of the night.

All in all, the goal was to make their time on *Sam's Place* comfortable, safe, and enjoyable, and it was good to be able to achieve these goals.

JERRY LEWIS FILMS INC.

INTER-OFFICE COMMUNICATION

TO: JOE PROULX

FROM: JL.

RE: "BOAT STUFF"

DATE: AUGUST 27.1990

CC. TO: REAL ADMIRAL NIMITZ(HE DIED! FORGET HIM)

DEAR JOE;

MOST OF THE FOLLOWING YOU ALREADY KNOW....BUT I'D LOVE GETTING SOME OF THIS TAKEN CARE OF (WE COME DOWN AGAIN ABOUT THE 13TH OF SEPT WITH THE GREENBERG'S)..

1...DUMP LADDERS TOPSIDE AND REMOVE WOOD HOLDERS....

2...RUN A.C. FROM BRASS LAMP IN MASTER TO BEHIND T.V.SET(AS DISCUSSED)

3...PAINT CREW'S QUARTERS AGAIN INCLUDING BUNKS....NEW LAMPS PUT IN...
   MAKE SURE IT'S THE SHINEY PAINT.....SAME IN HEAD AND GET NEW HARDWARE
   FOR CREW'S "HEAD"

4...CHROME LAST CLEAT AFT/PORT SIDE ABOVE TRANSOM...

5...REPLACE ALL GLASS IN WINDSHIELDS....(AFTER WOOD IS DONE(WE DISCUSSED
   THAT...IT JUST LOOKS SO TERRIBLE)

6...WINDSHIELD WIPERS......LET'S PUT A DETECTIVE ON IT AND FIND OUT WHERE
   IN GOD'S KETTINBURG CAN THEY BE FOUND...

7...REPLACE DOOR (WE HATE) THAT OPENS TO CONTROL LINES,AS YOU GO BELOW
   TO MASTER........

8...BRASS THE HANDRAILS GOING BELOW TO MASTER

9...THE HEAD LINERS ON BRIDGE ARE FILTHY AND SHOULD BE REPLACED....(WITH
   SOMETHING OTHER THAN 1960 HEADLINER)

10...BRIDGE SEAT(BATTERY AREA) NEEDS FRONT REPLACED.

11..HARDWARE FOR CREW'S HEAD

12..HARDWARE FOR PULL DOWN BUNK(IN GUEST STATEROOM) AND BULBS FOR TWIN
   LAMP.....UNDER PULL DOWN BUNK.

13..REPLACE ALL WALL HEATERS......(ARE THEY STANDARD???)
   (MASTER STATEROOM/GUEST STATEROOM/SALON/CREW'S QUARTERS/MASTER HEAD)

14..HEAD LINER(SALON)(AS DISCUSSED)(8 LIGHTS.....ONE ROW OF 3....ONE ROW
   OF 3 AND ONE ROW OF TWO......

JERRY LEWIS FILMS INC.

INTER-OFFICE COMMUNICATION

TO: _____ JOE PROULX-PAGE #2 _____

FROM:_____

RE: _____

DATE:_____

CC. TO:_____

15..PAINT INSIDES OF ALL CUPBOARDS AND CABINETS....

16..PAINT INTERIOR OF LAZERETTE

17..STEP FOR CAPT.ON BRIDGE TO SEE FOR DOCKING(SAME SIZE AS RUG BUT 4"
    HIGH)

18..FINISH CHROME OF ANCHOR WINCH(THE ONE HE CHROMED ONLY ONE SIDE.

19..NEW SCREENS PUT INTO STARBOARD AND PORT DOORS.

20..DUMP WATER SPICKET FROM STAR.SIDE AND REPLACE WITH CLEAT.

21..CAN WE USE A 2ND WATER HEATER???(WILL IT FIT???)

22..NEW DOOR AND HARDWARE FROM GALLEY TO CREW'S QUARTERS....

23..PAINT ENGINE ROOM(AS DISCUSSED)

24..SCRAPE AND VARNISH HAND RAILS OVER AND UNDER(ESPECIALLY AFT)

25..SCRAPE AND VARNISH WOOD ON BOW SEAT
    "" ""   " " " " " BRIDGE CABIN....

26..ALL WOOD NEEDS RE-DOING(BUT WE KNOW THAT!!!!!)

27..VARNISH BRIDGE THROUGH-OUT COVER ALL THE "V" MARKS CAPT.IDIOT PUT THEI

28..AL MALONE NOTES......(JOE HANDLE)

29..SILICONE WOULD HELP THE SLIDING WINDOWS IN THE MASTER STATEROOM
    THEY REALLY STICK!!!!

30..PAINT TOP OF BOAT "WHITE" AFTER LADDERS AND WOOD IS DUMPED...

31..PAINT ANTENNA(SHINEY WHITE)(BOTH OF THEM)

32..BRASS PLATES ON ALL MISSING A.C.OUTLETS..

33..REPAIR MIRROR CRACK ABOVE WALL HEATER IN MASTER

34..GLASS A.C. FOR "SAM'S" DRESSING TABLE(TO COVER THE MISSING A.C.PLATE)

35..CHROME "BROWN PLATES" ON OUTSIDE OF BOAT...(THERE ARE 2 OR 3)

JERRY LEWIS FILMS INC.

INTER-OFFICE COMMUNICATION

TO: _____ JOE PROULX-PAGE #3 _____

FROM: _____

RE: _____

DATE: _____

CC. TO: _____

36..DISCUSS WITH ME "MIRROR DOORS IN STATEROOM"(4)

37..PUSH SALLY FOR CURTAINS AND WHATEVER ELSE SHE'S DOING.

38..PAINT <u>STANTIO</u>NS GLOSSY WHITE!!!!

39..NEW LIFE LINES

40..WE SHOULD TALK ABOUT A NICE TEAK AND CHROME LADDER ON THE PORT SIDE
AFT OF TRANSOM(DOWN THE ROAD)

41..NOW THAT YOU'VE READ THE AFORGOING......TAKE A NAP AND BUY A COPY OF
"WAR AND PEACE"(YOU'LL GET THROUGH THAT SOONER)

LOVE TO SHIRLEY AND YOU FROM SAM AND ME....

REGARDS TO DON(IF HE'LL UNDERSTAND)

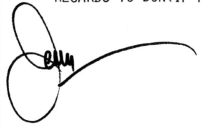

MEMO
5/14/98

JOE
I WANT
You TO
FEEL Right
AT Home —

Jerry Lewis

MEMO
9/24/90

Joe —

with this
Comes Jove
and Respect
Always
JL.

JERRY LEWIS

MEMO
9/13/91

JOE re:

EASE UP
STARBOARD
(2) WINDOWS
IN SALON —
HELP !!!

JERRY LEWIS

⚓ 140 ⚓

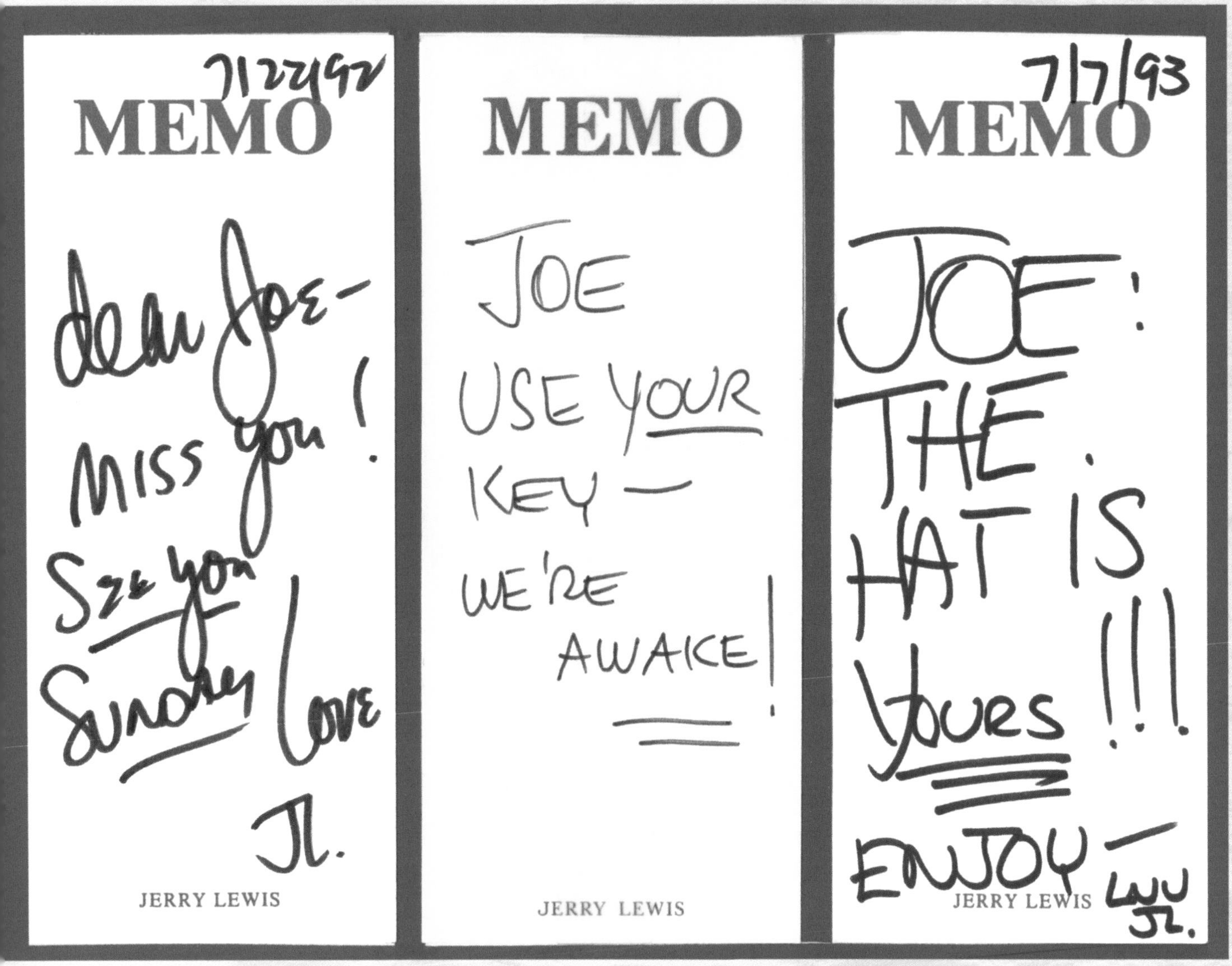

MEMO

7/22/92

dear Joe—
Miss you!
See you
Sunday love
JL.

JERRY LEWIS

MEMO

Joe
use your
KEY—
we're
awake!

JERRY LEWIS

MEMO

7/7/93

Joe!
THE.
HAT IS
Yours !!!
ENJOY—
love
JL.

JERRY LEWIS

A GENEROUS FELLOW

Jerry always returned to the boat after being on the road, bringing a gift for me and Shirley. Whether big or small, it was a touch of generosity indicative of a "giving" person. I always wear a beautiful watch he brought me from his last Australian tour.

Jerry really enjoyed shopping, happily coming back to the boat with an abundance of gifts or supplies. If we needed one item, he brought back 25, and I was tested to find storage for the excess. The photo below demonstrates how happy he must have made one store owner.

The results of one shopping trip!

CELEBRATING JERRY LEWIS'S 75ᵀᴴ
21

In March 2001, Sam planned a special celebration for Jerry's 75ᵗʰ birthday. Many friends were there, the decorations were beautiful, and his beloved yacht looked sparkling.

The phone rang off the hook with "Happy Birthday" wishes from all over the world – it was a beautiful tribute to his special day. He also received two huge albums of cards and letters from such celebrities as Andy Williams, Dr. Michael DeBakey, and film director Steven Spielberg. All the people associated with the Muscular Dystrophy Association and their many headquarters across the nation sent greetings.

~SHIRLEY

Jerry postures aboard *Sam's Place!*

The Lewis Family, Dani, Jerry, and Sam, enjoy great food and gifts.

Jerry opens one of many gifts.

Joe built a model Chris Craft Runabout for Jerry's special gift.

Claudia, Dani, Sam, Mandy, and Lloyd admire the runabout.

Shirlee Miller takes a look at Joe's model.

Joe, Jerry, and Rudi in Joe's remodeled aft deck.

The happy couple dances aboard.

Jerry exclaims over being "King of Comedy."

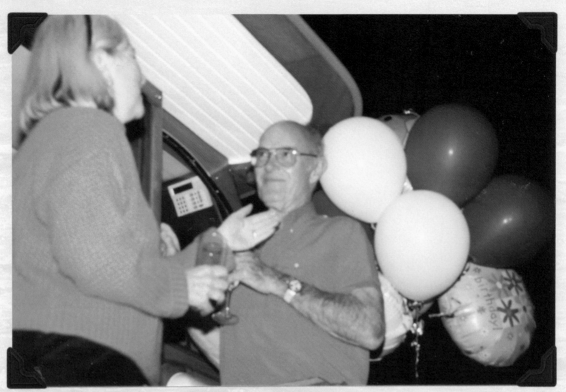

Shirlee Miller and Joe.

Rudi, Max Alexander, and Joe.

Fellow yachtsman Lloyd and "Comedy King" don festive crowns.

Sam and Jerry still happy after 18 years of marriage.

Jerry prepares to blow out the candles.

A FULFILLMENT FOR SAM

While I was still on the job, Sam began to take riding lessons in Del Mar. She developed a talent and love for these magnificent horses to fill her need for a much-needed escape from a demanding schedule.

Shirley and I were so happy to receive this photo she sent – many years after her initial effort, she had progressed to owning her own beautiful horse which she stabled in Las Vegas. She became an excellent rider, and we were glad to see she pursued her interest to achieve these goals – and that she shared her joy with us once again!

Sam hugs her beautiful horse, Gunner, in Las Vegas.

TIME TO SAY GOODBYE

In June 2001, I gave notice to Jerry that I would retire on my 78th birthday. I had experienced increasing difficulty in performing my duties. My usual level of ability was diminishing, especially when I tried to do jobs that required getting down on my knees. Those efforts caused pain and irritability. My wife, Shirley, had retired the year before when she sold her printing company.

Jerry was going through serious health problems of his own – one of the most serious was a viral lung infection that required treatment with the drug Prednisone – a very tough treatment with all kinds of adverse side effects. He was also in considerable pain, suffering from the effect of the many pratfalls he took over the years.

We made quite a pair!

In November 2001, Sam and Claudia put on a dock party for me and some of our friends: Rudi, Mandy and Lloyd, Liz and Joe (Claudia's sister and brother-in-law), and Paco, my valued deck hand, who helped with the delicious food that was served. Jerry couldn't attend because of poor health, and it was a sad occasion, in that respect. An important and very meaningful part of my life was over.

The following month, Shirley and I sold our San Diego property and moved to our retirement destination, Sedona, Arizona, where our new home was under construction. It was a unique and excellent retirement choice for many reasons. I got my knees replaced and felt better than I had in a very long time. I missed my friend Jerry, my job, and the interaction of my many friends. Born in San Diego, I will always think of it as home.

At this writing, I'm 91 years old, and I feel my decisions were good, under the circumstances. But I wouldn't mind reporting for duty on *Sam's Place* in my heart!

Claudia, Joe, and Paco on the dock at my retirement party.

Joe and Paco share a laugh.

We say goodbye to *Sam's Place*.

Sam, Mandy, Rudi, Lloyd, Liz, and Joe – (Shirley's taking the pictures).

Jerry and I in November 2001, one of the last times on his yacht. I'm headed for retirement at 78!

Since I retired in 2001, I have talked with Cap'n. Queeg on the phone, and received notes and items of interest that he sends to include me "in the loop."

In 2010, I received an announcement of Dani's graduation from high school, and a lovely picture of a beautiful young lady who was preparing to go off to college. It was great to see our Dani again in her graduation portrait, and Shirley and I wish her every success and happiness.

We wanted to share our joy and pride with you...

Now onward and upward to Chapman University!

Love,
Sam & Jerry

In October 2013, my daughter, Cheryl, and husband, Ed, gave me a 90th birthday party at their Pacific Beach home., with some 50 people in attendance. It was a beautiful, first-rate affair (they give splendid parties!), and then came the icing on the cake: Jerry Lewis walked in as a special surprise! He had flown in from Las Vegas especially to wish me a "Happy Birthday" – personally. There wasn't a dry eye in the house. Jac and Mary Lou Flanders accompanied him, and it was good to see them after so many years. It was truly an act of love on Jerry's part, and I shall always treasure that memory.

Joe tries to blow out his "bonfire."

Jerry deadpans to Joe and Shirley's delight.

My surprise guest, Jerry Lewis, who signed his picture for me "Joe Baby."

Over the many years I had the privilege to spend time with Jerry, both professionally and privately I enjoyed the many facets of his great talents and spontaneous wit and personality. It is indeed rare to see someone with so much talent in so many different areas.

I saw demonstrations of his photographic memory. Sometimes he asked a person for a piece of currency (bill). He glanced at it for a moment, gave it back to the owner, and reeled off the serial number – perfectly.

When aboard one of his vessels, one of his great jobs was to install chrome finish washers, which created a rich sparkling finish to the boat.

During a Sunday outing to the Coronado Hotel, he approached and sat next to a rather severe-looking older woman in the lobby. He put his arm around the back of the couch and proceeded to mimic her expressions, much to the amusement of the audience who had gathered to watch his antics. She was probably the best "straight" man he had ever appeared with – she never cracked a smile and I never found out if she was even aware of him being next to her!

One of his favorite tricks was to twirl up a napkin, put a pat of butter in the middle, give a quick jerk on the two ends, and sail the butter up to the ceiling – an extraordinary feat that always drew laughs. He also pretended to bend silverware, put whole glassware into his mouth, and clown around with whichever object would get a laugh.

He was very capable of a good cry and was easily touched by the pain of others. He wasn't embarrassed to show that he cared.

And if you weren't lucky enough to see his "cane" routine in "Damn Yankees," you've really missed something. It was masterful – a song and dance routine reminiscent of vaudeville, in which he tapped, threw, and caught his cane in many postures and rhythms.

He gifted me and my family with many keepsake photos and show-business items that I treasure. I am happy that I can share some of these with you, due to his generosity in allowing me to reprint his professional photos, as well as our personal photos. This will give you a chance to learn more about this vibrant, slightly eccentric, and completely loveable man of so many talents.

My deepest thanks, Cap'n. Queeg, a.k.a. Jerry Lewis.

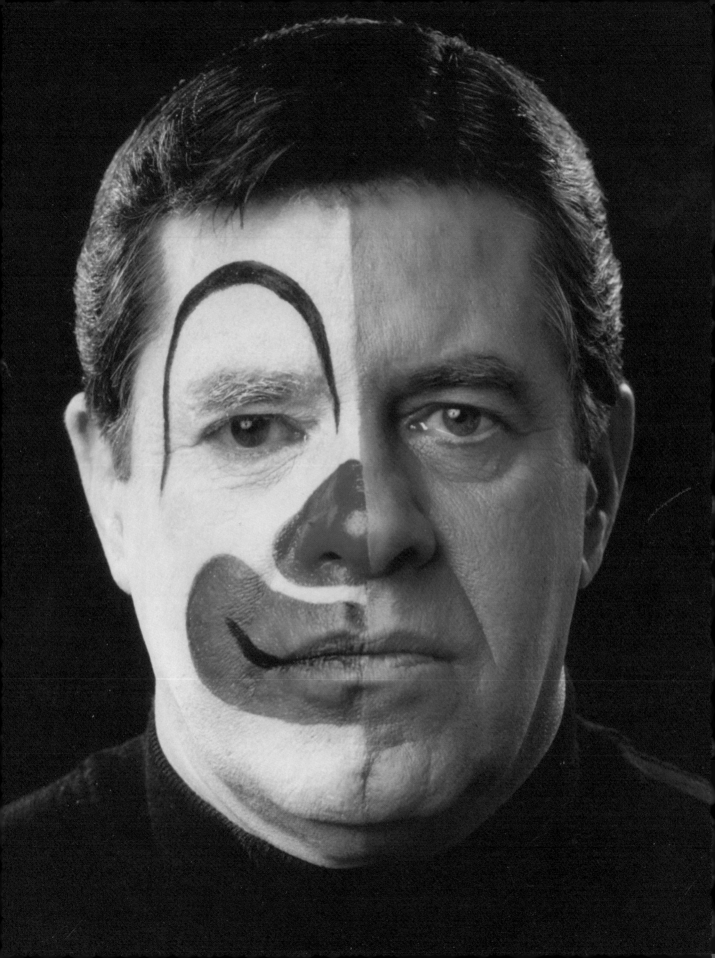

SUPPORTING CAST and FRIENDS

A number of Jerry Lewis's impressive staff played a key support role for me as Captain of his yacht. I could not have functioned in that capacity without their help. Here are the major players:

Joe and Claudia Stabile – Joe was Jerry's long-time manager, and was frequently with Jerry when he came to the boat, both for business and pleasure. Claudia took over Joe's responsibilities after his death, and was a remarkable source of support and the best darn cook, whether for two or 50 without batting an eye – amazing.

Violet Ostrow and Penny Rice – Jerry's long-time office staff. Vi controlled the purse strings and everything associated with funds and their dispensation. Penny kept us supplied with gifts to guests and friends, including photos and autographs. Both of these capable ladies worked long busy hours, especially during the Muscular Dystrophy Telethon. Thank you both, for all your help.

Jeff Lowe – a strong and efficient member of Jerry's staff – able to clear tall buildings at a single bound, or at least lift them. He was there delivering, lifting, organizing supplies and props. Thanks, Jeff, for your help and for sharing your adorable kids' pictures every Christmas.

Jac and Mary Lou Flanders – long-time friends of Jerry. Jac photographed many events and special times we shared as onboard guests. Thanks for including us at your Thanksgiving dinner. We'll never forget your "secret recipe" of *corn soufflé*.

Rudi Enners – fellow boat owner and friend – full of fun, humor, and often our traveling companion, especially during the New York and Telethon trips.

Dyan Allen – full of creative ideas. She suggested this book, and her enthusiasm kept the project moving forward.

Anne Crosman – adding her expertise as a published author to encourage and support our efforts. She also edited this book.

Newell Tarrant – our friend of many years and published author, who gave helpful and loving guidance, including suggesting this book's title. I wish we had his command of the English language!

Judy and Don Schwartzmiller – who gave us a little book *Shimmering Images* about writing memoirs.

Bill Johnson – who gave generously of his time and talent to help Shirley work on the computer program and picture quality.

Naomi Rose – our designer, who became so much more during the book's creation. She not only offered her considerable talent and guidance, but also expressed her enthusiasm and excitement over the project. Her positive attitude was a much-appreciated support for us. She carefully guided us and worked to help us achieve our budget goals.

Erica Patstone – an award-winning student majoring in Graphic Design at Cal Poly in San Luis Obispo and working part-time, also helped us lay out our book using InDesign. She worked diligently for us with all the demands of her busy schedule. We want to wish her every success in her chosen field, and thank her for all her efforts.

Pat Gresham Nuckols – our dear friend of many years, who passed away last November. She generously enabled us to create and share Joe's story.

SPECIAL THANKS TO OUR FAMILY, who encouraged us and offered their help. We're especially grateful to Susan Moore, Shirley's daughter, who held our hands throughout the process, and patiently dealt with our limited computer skills. Susan offered her significant background in the printing industry to guide our efforts. Cheryl Nodland, Joe's eldest daughter and her husband, Ed, who spent hours guiding us through technical steps of putting our stories and pictures on paper correctly. THANKS, KIDS!

CPSIA information can be obtained at www.ICGtesting.com
Printed in the USA
BVIW12n1236040118
504333BV00016B/255